Looking into Literature and Seeing Myself

Primary Literature and Research Activities to Help Young Children Learn About Themselves

by
Laurie Chapin and Ellen Flegenheimer-Riggle

illustrated by Laurie Chapin

Cover by Jeff Van Kanegan

Copyright © Good Apple, 1992
ISBN No. 0-86653-706-6
Printing No. 987654321

Good Apple
1204 Buchanan Street, Box 299
Carthage, IL 62321-0299

S I M O N & S C H U S T E R *A Paramount Communications Company*

Dedicated

with love to
our siblings

Carol

Lori

Eric

and

Mark . . .

Special thanks to
Kimberly Cloud
Mari Beth Jennings Hall

GA1427

Table of Contents

GA1427

Suggestions for Using This Book

Bloom's Questions

- Select all or some of the questions and activities for a whole group discussion, small group or paired discussion or independent study.

- Create a comfortable atmosphere by accepting answers in a nonjudgmental manner.

Tell about something special you would share with a new friend.

- Allow children ample time to respond to each question.

- Allow active participation from many children.

- Use blank shapes for making Bloom's Question cards. (See Blank Shapes directions.)

- Use blank shapes for recording children's individual responses to Bloom's Questions.

Creative Thinking Activities

- Be accepting of all answers.

- Allow adequate discussion time for brainstorming to become fruitful.

- Allow adequate "wait time" for each answer.

- Create a class "Brainstorming Book" to record fluency activities. (Use large lined chart paper. Glue wrapping paper on the front for a colorful cover.)

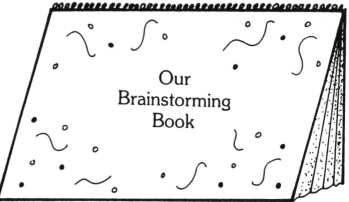

Our Brainstorming Book

- Use blank shapes for making Creative Thinking Activities cards. (See Blank Shapes directions.)

- Use blank shapes for recording children's individual responses to Creative Thinking Activities.

GA1427

Blank Shapes

- Reproduce blank shapes to make shape cards. Print the questions and activities on them. Use one question per shape. Laminate and assemble cards on a ring.

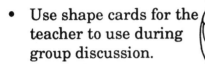

- Use shape cards for the teacher to use during group discussion.

- Use shape cards for the children to use with a partner, school volunteer or for independent study.

- Use shape cards at a learning center. Display them with the book and activity sheets.

- Use shapes for a class book or an individual student's book.

- Reproduce shapes for children to record individual thoughts.

- Use shapes to create a bulletin board display.

Activity Sheets

- An asterisk designates written or illustrated activities that include activity sheets.

- Use activity sheets as a bulletin board display.

- Use activity sheets to create a class book.

- Assemble by laminating a colorful cover.

- Attach students' work with:
  - plastic spiral binding
  - hole punch with notebook ring or yarn
  - staple

People Poll - Graphing

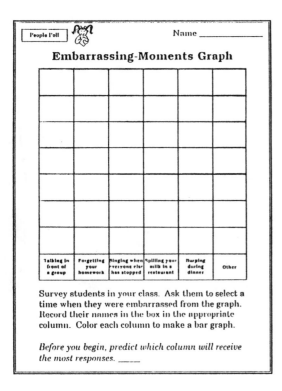

- Involve students actively in completing the graphs.

- Use graphs to collect and analyze data.

- Use graphs to survey students, school personnnel and/or friends.

- Discuss graph results as a whole group, small group, or paired discussion.

- Allow students to develop graphs of their own.

- Use graphs as a classroom display.

Home-School Research

- Use research activities to build a home-school connection.

- Use research activities to help students better understand themselves, families, and friends.

- Allow children to take research activities home to discuss with family members.

- Encourage students to use their creative thinking skills to add unique and colorful details to their final research products.

- Share the research activities as a whole group, small group, or paired discussion.

- Display research activities as a bulletin board or other classroom display.

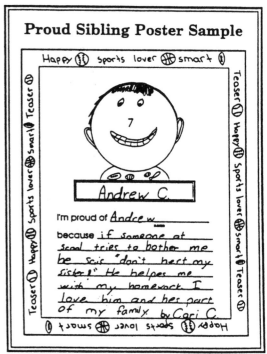

GA1427

CHRISTINA KATERINA AND THE TIME SHE QUIT THE FAMILY

Patricia Lee Gauch
G.P. Putnam's Sons, NY, 1987

Christina Katerina quits her family and does exactly as she pleases. No one can tell her what to do.

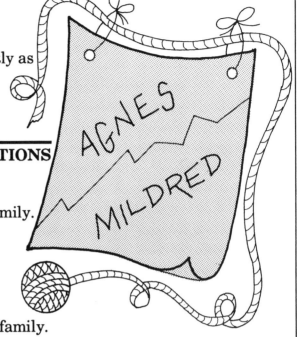

BLOOM'S QUESTIONS

KNOWLEDGE
Name the members of Christina Katerina's family.

COMPREHENSION
Why did Christina Katerina quit the family?

APPLICATION
Share a time when you felt like quitting your family.

ANALYSIS
Examine the activities Christina Katerina does when she is Agnes. How are they different from activities she is allowed to do when she is Christina?

SYNTHESIS
Predict what Christina Katerina would have done if her mother had not brought her the chocolate cake.

EVALUATION
Decide what lesson Christina Katerina learned in the family.

CREATIVE THINKING ACTIVITIES

FLUENCY
Make a long list of things that you like about your family.

FLEXIBILITY
Select three items from your list that are unique about your family. Select three items from your list that are common to many families.

*ORIGINALITY
Christina Katerina made a peanut butter and potato chip sandwich for supper. Create a day's menu for Agnes. Make your selections interesting.

*ELABORATION
Add details to Christina Katerina's sign at the end of the story.

GA1427

CHRISTINA KATERINA AND THE TIME SHE QUIT THE FAMILY

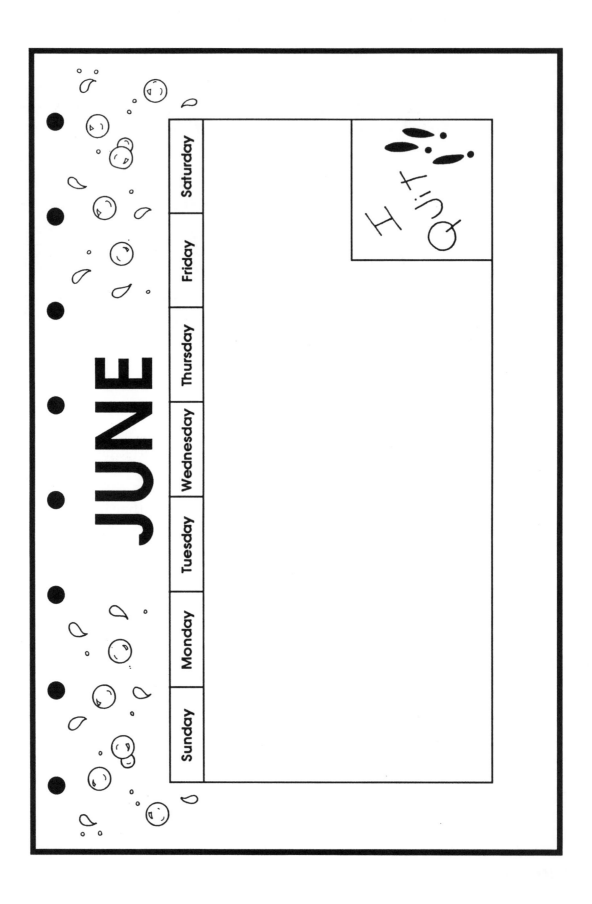

JUNE

Sunday	Monday	Tuesday	Wednesday	Thursday	Friday	Saturday

GA1427

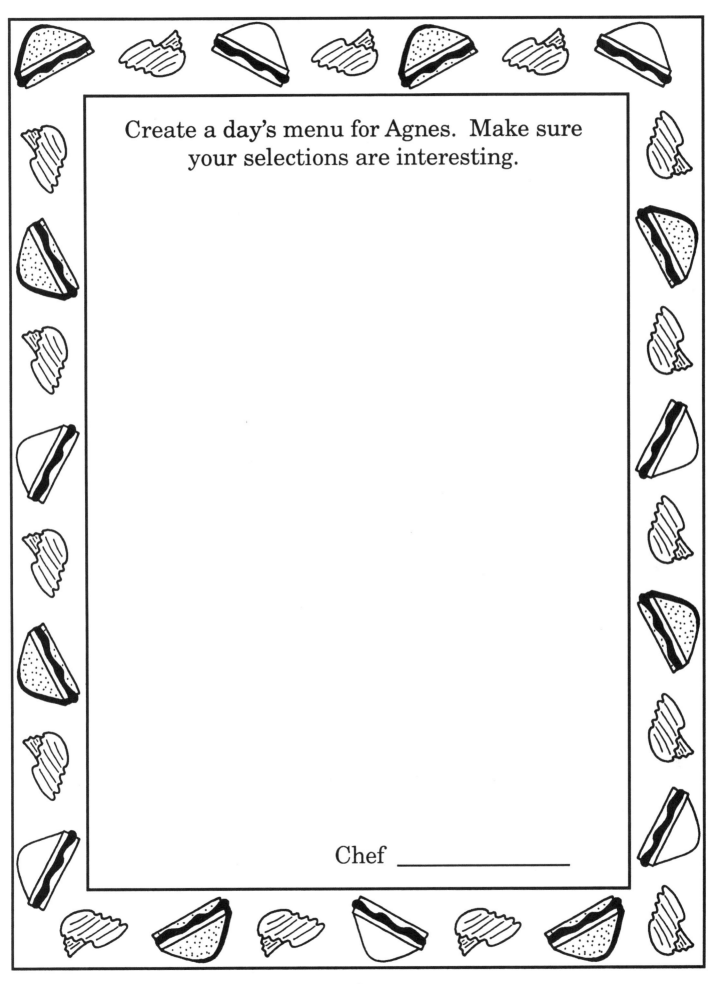

Create a day's menu for Agnes. Make sure
your selections are interesting.

Chef _____

GA1427

Add details to Christina Katerina's sign at the end of the story.

CHRISTINA KATERINA LIVES HERE!

Sign Maker _____

4

Name _____

What-Would-You-Miss Graph

My parent's cooking						
Bedtime stories						
Playing with siblings						
Special celebra- tions						
Family trips						
Hugs and kisses						
Other						

Survey students in your classroom. What would they miss the most if they quit their families? Record their names in the box in the appropriate column. Color each column to make a bar graph.

Before you begin, predict which column will receive the most responses. _____

Name _____

Exploring the What-Would-You-Miss Graph

1. Which column had the most responses?_____
   _____

2. Which column had the least responses?_____
   _____

3. Were there any ties?_____
   _____

4. What conclusions can you make from your graph?_____
   _____
   _____
   _____
   _____

5. Did students have difficulty selecting only one thing they would miss about their families?_____

6. Share five things you would miss about your family. Be specific.

   1._____
   2._____
   3._____
   4._____
   5._____

GA1427

School

HOME-SCHOOL RESEARCH
Family Bug-a-Boos

Home
Sweet
Home

DIRECTIONS: You are going to discover what things bug your family members. Ask each family member to share one thing that bugs him/her about the family. Record the responses in the bug below. Select three bug-a-boos and write their solutions on the Family Bug-a-Boo page.

GA1427

Family Bug-a-Boos

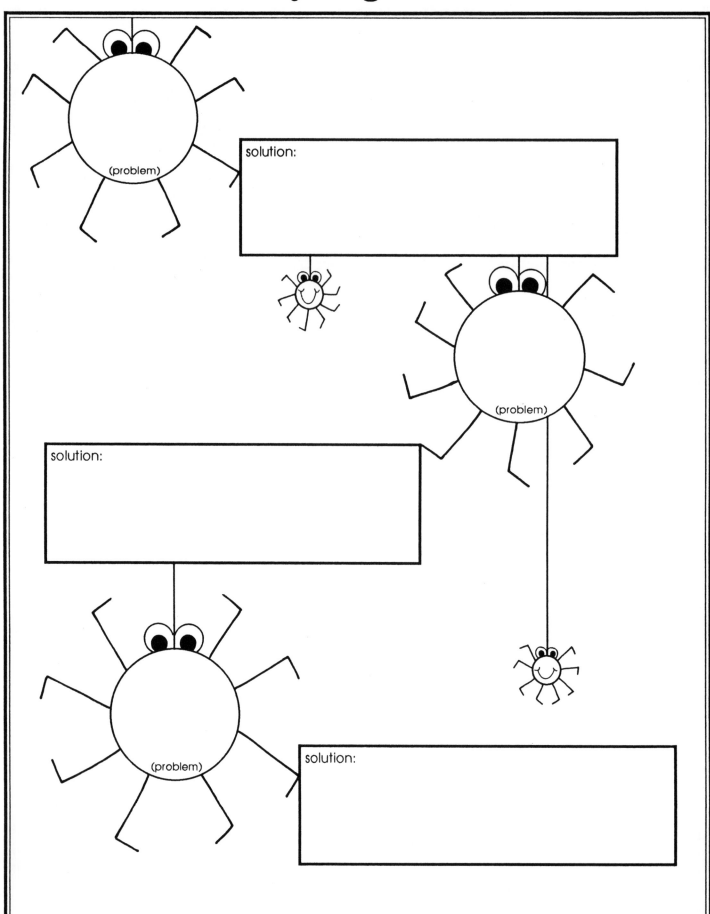

(problem)

solution:

(problem)

solution:

(problem)

solution:

GA1427

DADDY HAS A PAIR OF STRIPED SHORTS

Mimi Otey
Farrar, Straus and Giroux, NY, 1990

A little girl's father has real difficulty selecting clothes that match, but only his family seems to notice.

BLOOM'S QUESTIONS

KNOWLEDGE
What is the daddy's job in the story?

COMPREHENSION
Explain how the little girl felt about her daddy's clothes.

APPLICATION
Share an experience when you felt embarrassed.

ANALYSIS
Compare the daddy's clothes in the story with your daddy's clothes. How are they the same? How are they different?

*SYNTHESIS
Create a new outfit for Daddy. Make it as unusual as you can.

EVALUATION
Should Daddy be judged by the clothes he wears? Should other people be judged by the clothes they wear? Tell why or why not.

CREATIVE THINKING ACTIVITIES

FLUENCY
The little girl discovers how much she appreciates her daddy in the story. Make a long list of things you appreciate.

*FLEXIBILITY
Think of a different use for one of daddy's jackets in the story.

ORIGINALITY
Write a letter to someone you appreciate. Be sure to tell him/her why he/she is appreciated.

ELABORATION
Elaborate on a tie for Daddy. Add as many details as you can.

GA1427

DADDY HAS A PAIR OF STRIPED SHORTS

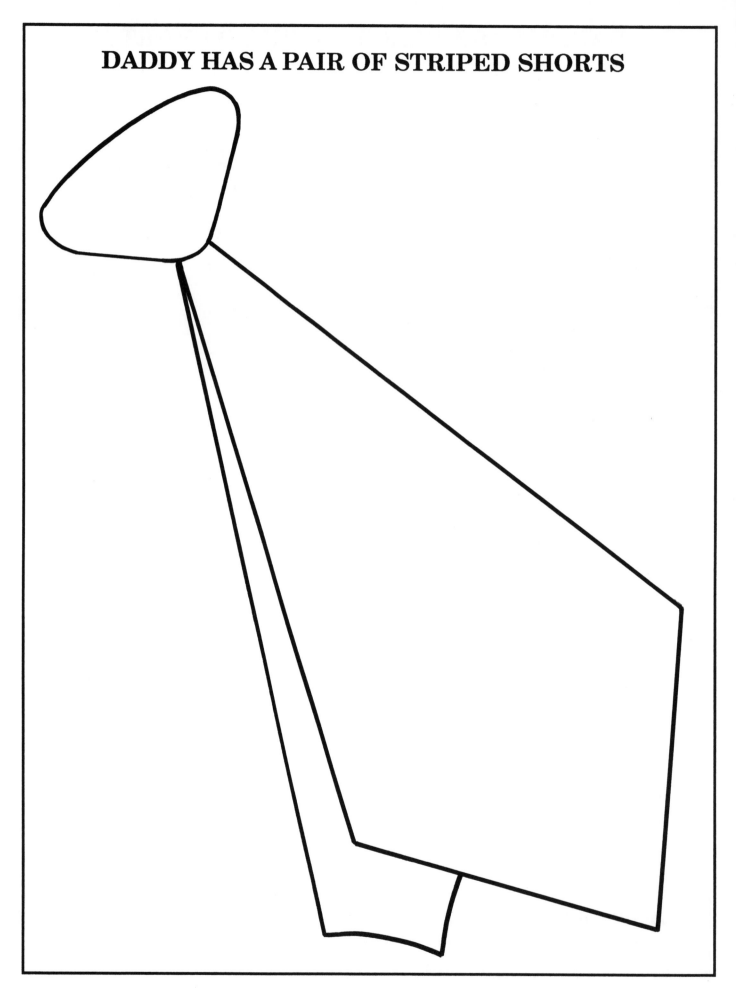

10

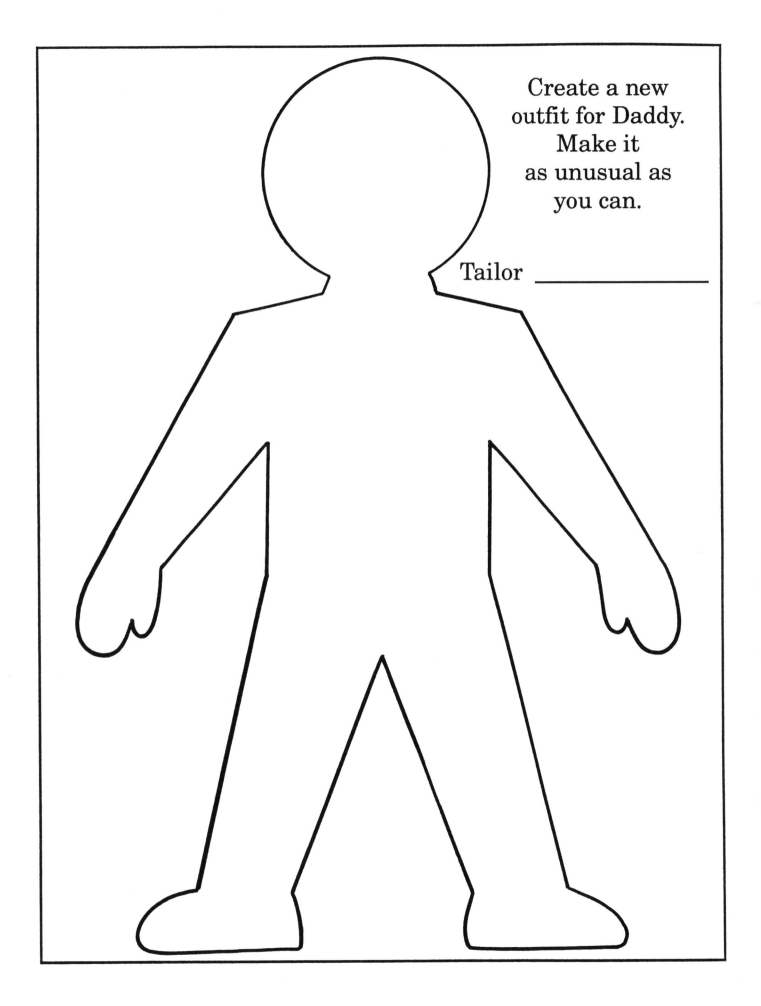

Create a new
outfit for Daddy.
Make it
as unusual as
you can.

Tailor _____

11

GA1427

Think of a different use for one
of Daddy's jackets in the story.

Creative Jacket Recycler _____

Name _____

Embarrassing-Moments Graph

Talking in front of a group	Forgetting your homework	Singing when everyone else has stopped	Spilling your milk in a restaurant	Burping during dinner	Other

Survey students in your class. Ask them to select a time when they were embarrassed from the graph. Record their names in the box in the appropriate column. Color each column to make a bar graph.

Before you begin, predict which column will receive the most responses. _____

GA1427

Exploring the Embarrassing-Moments Graph

1. Which column had the most responses?_____
   _____

2. Which column had the least responses?_____
   _____

3. Were there any ties?_____
   _____

4. What other embarrassing moments did your class-mates share with you?_____
   _____
   _____
   _____

5. Brainstorm a solution for an embarrassing moment.
   _____
   _____
   _____
   _____

14

GA1427

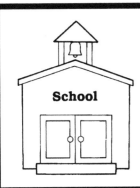
School

HOME-SCHOOL RESEARCH
Starring My Dad

Home
Sweet
Home

DIRECTIONS: You are going to discover your dad's star qualities. Discuss these qualities with your mom, siblings, and other
relatives . . . but keep them a secret from your dad. Write these
traits on the marquee below. Using the star form provided, create a ribbon for your dad.

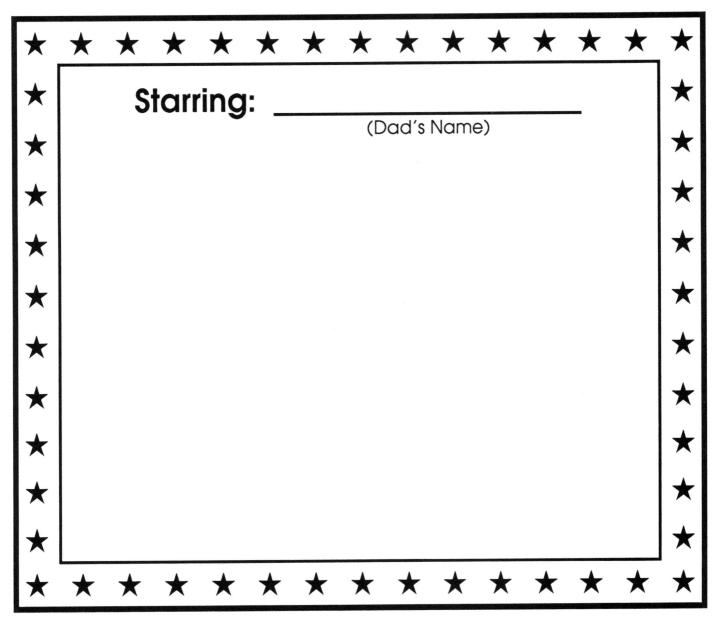

Starring: _____
(Dad's Name)

GA1427

Select five of your dad's star qualities and write one in each point of the star. Decorate your star ribbon and present it to your dad.

My Dad

_____

(Dad's Name)

16

THE HATING BOOK

Charlotte Zolotow
Harper & Row, NY, 1969

One young girl "hate hates" her friend and struggles with how to resolve her feelings.

BLOOM'S QUESTIONS

KNOWLEDGE
List three reasons why the little girl "hate hated" her friend.

COMPREHENSION
Why did the little girl follow her mom's advice?

APPLICATION
What do you do when you have a disagreement with your friend?

ANALYSIS
Analyze how the disagreement between the little girls could have been avoided.

SYNTHESIS
Write a letter asking for advice about a real or pretend problem. (Collect the letters and distribute among the class to answer.)

EVALUATION
Was the mother's advice to the little girl good? Tell why or why not.

CREATIVE THINKING ACTIVITIES

FLUENCY
Brainstorm reasons why friends get angry with each other.

*FLEXIBILITY
Draw a picture of another way the little girl could have resolved her problem.

*ORIGINALITY
Write about a "best" friend. Tell about what you like to do together, why he/she is special, and how you are alike and different (brainstorm possible ideas as a class).

ELABORATION
Elaborate on the end of the story. What do you think the two young girls will do tomorrow?

GA1427

THE HATING BOOK

18

Draw a picture of another way the little
girl could have resolved her problem.

Problem Solver _____

MY BEST FRIEND

My best friend's full name is _____

_____

We are alike because _____

_____

_____

We are different because _____

_____

_____

Together we like to _____

_____

_____

Once I felt angry with my friend because _____

_____

_____

My best friend is special to me because _____

_____

_____

_____

_____

Friend _____

GA1427

Name _____

Becoming-Friends-Again Graph

Saying I'm sorry	Writing a note	Giving someone a hug	Making something special for someone	Calling on the phone	Doing or saying something nice	Other

Survey people in your school. What way do they think is the best way to "become friends again" after a disagreement? Record their names in the box in the appropriate column. Color each column to make a bar graph.

Before you begin, predict which column will receive the most responses. _____

21

GA1427

Name _____

Exploring the Becoming-
Friends-Again Graph

1. Which column had the most responses?_____
   _____

2. Which column had the least responses?_____
   _____

3. Were there any ties?_____
   _____

4. What conclusions can you make from your graph?_____
   _____
   _____
   _____
   _____

5. Share a time when you were angry with your friend
   and tell how you became friends again._____
   _____
   _____
   _____
   _____
   _____

GA1427

HOME-SCHOOL RESEARCH
Wanted: a Best Friend

School

Home Sweet Home

DIRECTIONS: You are searching for a best friend. Brainstorm the qualities and/or interests you would like in an ideal best friend. Write your ideas in the brainstorming box below. Using the Wanted poster provided, write a description of your ideal best friend and draw a picture of him or her.

My family's brainstorming list of best friend qualities:

GA1427

WANTED

. . . a Best Friend . . .

_____

_____

_____

_____

_____

_____

_____

_____

_____

_____

_____

_____

_____

_____

_____

_____

_____

_____

_____

_____

_____

_____

_____

_____

JULIUS • THE BABY OF THE WORLD

Kevin Henkes
Greenwillow Books, NY, 1990

Julius is "the baby of the world." But Lilly, the older
sister, disagrees and thinks Julius should go away.

BLOOM'S QUESTIONS

KNOWLEDGE
Name three things Lilly does not like about Julius.

COMPREHENSION
What is the real reason Lilly doesn't like Julius?

APPLICATION
Lilly was jealous of Julius. Share a time in your life when you felt jealous.

ANALYSIS
Decide how Lilly felt when it became apparent that Cousin Garland didn't like
Julius.

*SYNTHESIS
Create a book of ideas to help someone become a better brother or sister.

EVALUATION
Decide whether Lilly is a good big sister to Julius. Explain your answer.

CREATIVE THINKING ACTIVITIES

FLUENCY
Brainstorm as many reasons as you can why babies cry.

*FLEXIBILITY
When Julius grows up he will no longer need his crib. Think of another use for the
crib.

ORIGINALITY
Suppose Julius could talk to Lilly. What would he say to her?

ELABORATION
At the end of the story, Lilly declares that "JULIUS IS THE BABY OF THE
WORLD." Elaborate on what things Lilly and Julius will do together in the future.

GA1427

JULIUS • THE BABY OF THE WORLD

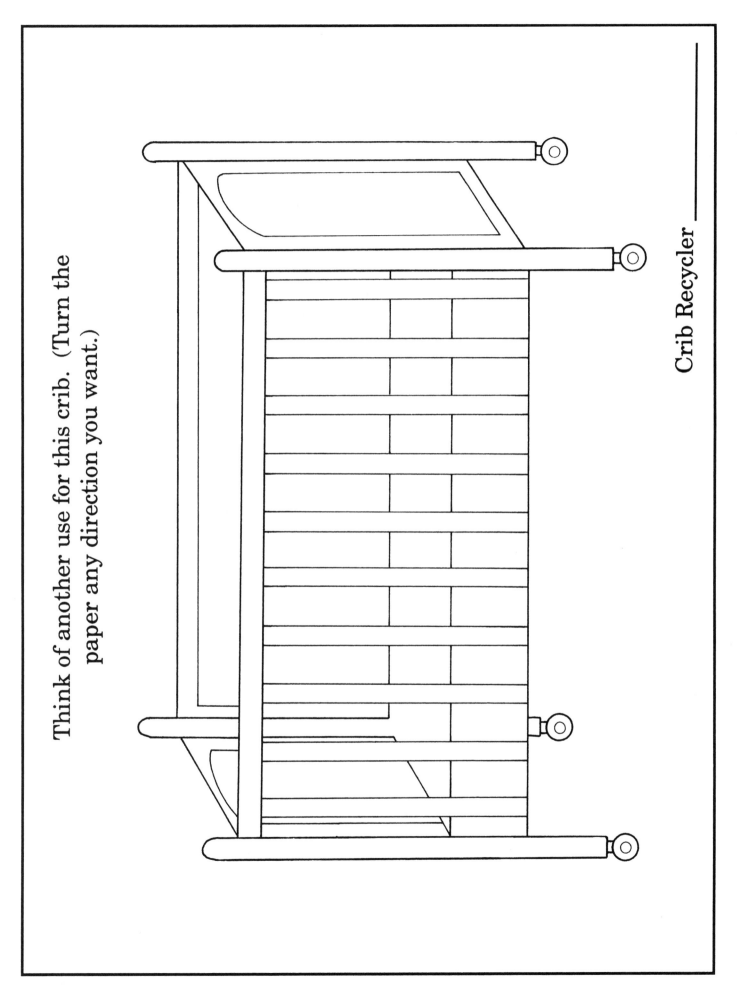

Think of another use for this crib. (Turn the paper any direction you want.)

Crib Recycler

27

GA1427

Write a "How to Be a Better Brother or Sister Advice Book." Complete the pages below and assemble as a small booklet.

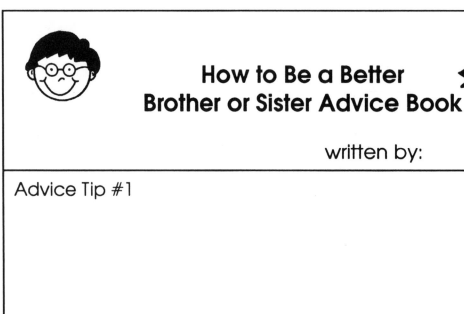

How to Be a Better Brother or Sister Advice Book

written by:

Advice Tip #1

Advice Tip #2

Advice Tip #3

Advice Tip #4

Name _____

Sibling Graph

0	**1**	**2**	**3** or more

Survey people in your school. How many siblings do they have? Record their names in the box in the appropriate column. Color each column to make a bar graph.

Before you begin, predict which column will receive the most responses. _____

Name _____

Exploring the Sibling Graph

1. Which column had the most responses?_____
    _____

2. Which column had the least responses?_____
    _____

3. Were there any ties?_____
    _____

4. What conclusions can you make from your graph?____
    _____
    _____
    _____
    _____

5. Something I learned that the graph doesn't show: ____
    _____
    _____
    _____

6. Bonus: Tell about your own siblings.
    How many siblings do you have?_____
    Brothers?_____   Older?_____
    Sisters?_____   Younger?_____
    Interesting facts about your siblings:_____
    _____

HOME-SCHOOL RESEARCH
A Parade of Siblings

School

Home Sweet Home

DIRECTIONS: You are the proud sibling of a brother and/or sister. Interview one of your siblings and gather information to complete the form below. Then make a poster about your sibling. 1. Use the description to draw a picture of your sibling. 2. Write the personality traits of your sibling in the border using a pattern that repeats. 3. Complete the "I'm Proud of My Sibling" statement below the picture. Mount and display your poster in your classroom as "A Proud Parade of Siblings."

Sibling Interview

Name of Sibling: _____

Description of Sibling: _____

_____

Personality Traits (at least four): _____

_____

Reasons I'm Proud of My Sibling: _____

_____

_____

_____

_____

_____

GA1427

Proud Sibling Poster Layout

I'm proud of _____
                    (name)

because _____

_____

_____

_____

_____

_____

LEO THE LATE BLOOMER

Robert Kraus
Windmill Books, NY, 1971

Leo couldn't do anything right. Leo's parents watched for signs of change and slowly watched him "bloom."

BLOOM'S QUESTIONS

KNOWLEDGE
Describe Leo.

COMPREHENSION
What does it mean to be "a late bloomer"?

APPLICATION
Share a time from your own life when you had difficulty doing something. How did you feel?

ANALYSIS
Compare yourself with Leo. How are you the same? How are you different?

*SYNTHESIS
Design a T-shirt for Leo offering words of encouragement.

EVALUATION
Decide if it was a good idea for Leo's parents to simply wait patiently for Leo to bloom. Why or why not?

CREATIVE THINKING ACTIVITIES

FLUENCY
Make a long list of tasks that are "difficult" for a child your age to accomplish.

FLEXIBILITY
Look at your list of tasks. Estimate how much time it will take to complete each task.

*ORIGINALITY
Draw a picture following the technique Leo used to write.

ELABORATION
Elaborate on the meaning of "a watched bloomer doesn't bloom."

GA1427

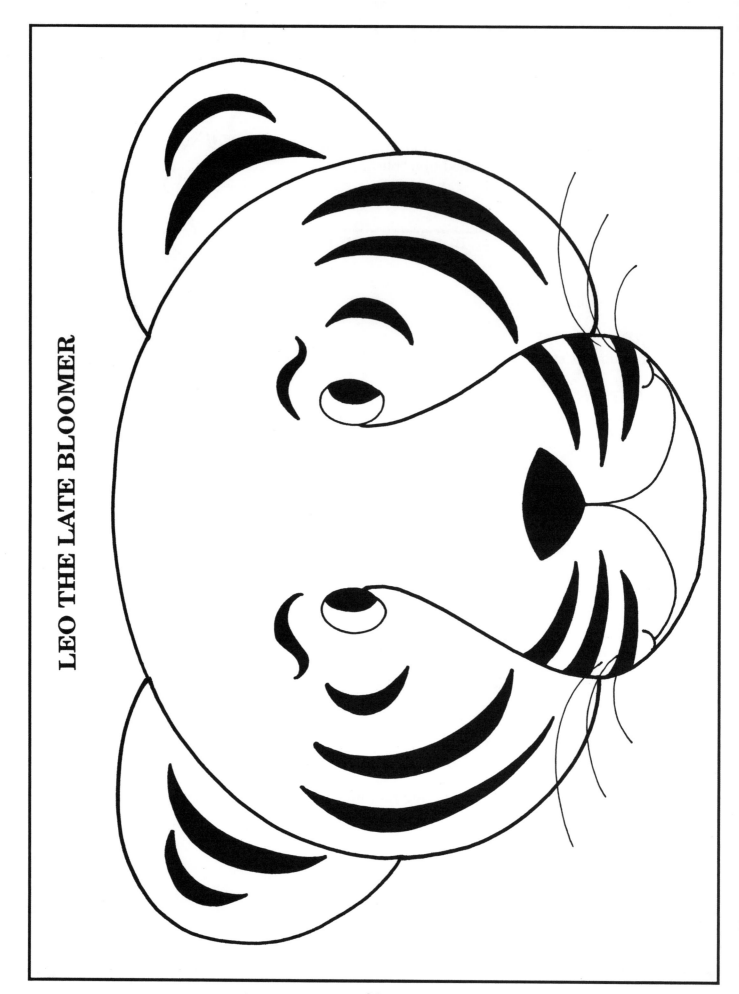

LEO THE LATE BLOOMER

34

Design a T-shirt for Leo offering
words of encouragement.

T-shirt Designer _____

Draw a picture following the technique
Leo used to write.

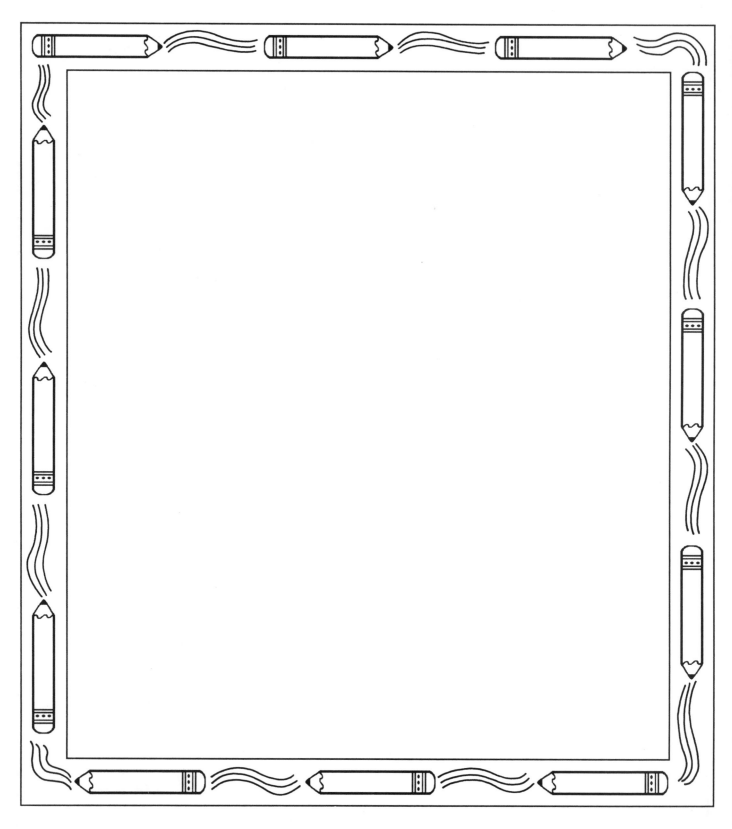

Artist _____

36

Name _____

Milestone Graph

Learning to read	Learning to write	Learning to ride a bike	Learning to tie a shoe	Learning to count to 100	Other

Survey students in your school. What do they consider the greatest milestone in their lives thus far? Record their names in the box in the appropriate column. Color each column to make a bar graph.

Before you begin, predict which column will receive the most responses. _____

GA1427

Name _____

Exploring the Milestone Graph

1. Which column had the most responses?_____
   _____

2. Which column had the least responses?_____
   _____

3. Were there any ties?_____
   _____

4. What conclusions can you make from your graph?_____
   _____
   _____
   _____
   _____

5. Bonus Question: Predict the greatest milestone for
   each of the ages listed below:

   one year old _____

   five years old _____

   ten years old _____

   sixteen years old _____

   twenty-five years old _____

   fifty years old _____

GA1427

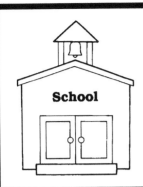

School

HOME-SCHOOL RESEARCH
A "Hooray for Me" Celebration

Home
Sweet
Home

DIRECTIONS: Leo bloomed and everyone celebrated. You are going to plan a celebration for an accomplishment in your life. The celebration could be for learning to read, tying your shoe, learning to ride a bike, scoring a goal in a soccer game, etc. Write your ideas for your celebration in the banner below. Then using the "Hooray for Me" page, create a special celebration day just for you.

REASONS I COULD CELEBRATE

1. _____

 because _____

2. _____

because _____

3. _____

because _____

4. _____

because _____

(Select your favorite accomplishment.)

GA1427

HOORAY FOR ME

A

_____

Celebration

I am celebrating _____ because _____
_____
_____

My celebration foods will be:

One game I will play at my celebration is:

I will invite these people to my celebration:

At my celebration, I will wear:

Some of my celebration decorations will be:

Other celebration ideas:

40

MAX

Rachel Isadora
Collier Books, NY, 1976

Max is a great baseball player who discovers that ballet
is a terrific way to get in shape for hitting a home run.

BLOOM'S QUESTIONS

KNOWLEDGE
Name three things Max does at the ballet lesson.

COMPREHENSION
How did Max become interested in the ballet school?

APPLICATION
Max was good at baseball and ballet. List two things that you do well.

ANALYSIS
Compare baseball with ballet. How are they the same? How are they different?

*SYNTHESIS
Suppose Max wants to be in the ballet recital. Draw a picture of Max wearing his
costume. (He cannot be a baseball player.)

EVALUATION
Was it a good idea for Max to go to dancing class? Why or why not?

CREATIVE THINKING ACTIVITIES

FLUENCY
Brainstorm as many types of sports as you can. Begin your list with baseball.

FLEXIBILITY
Look at your list of sports. Divide your list into as many categories as you can. For
example: sports using racquets, sports using balls, sports requiring a team, etc.

ORIGINALITY
Create a poster of yourself as the star of your favorite out-of-school activity.

*ELABORATION
Look closely at the black and white illustrations in the book. Elaborate on Max's
baseball cap. Add details and lots of color.

GA1427

MAX

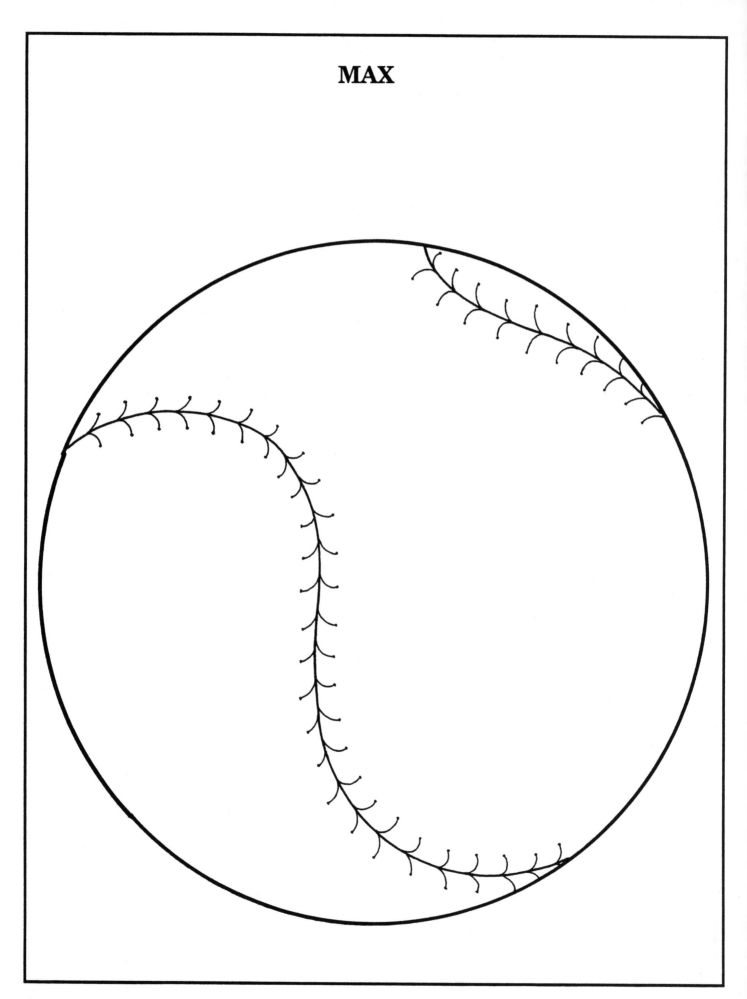

42

Draw a picture of Max in his recital costume.

Costume Creator _____

GA1427

Add designs and color to Max's baseball cap. Be creative!

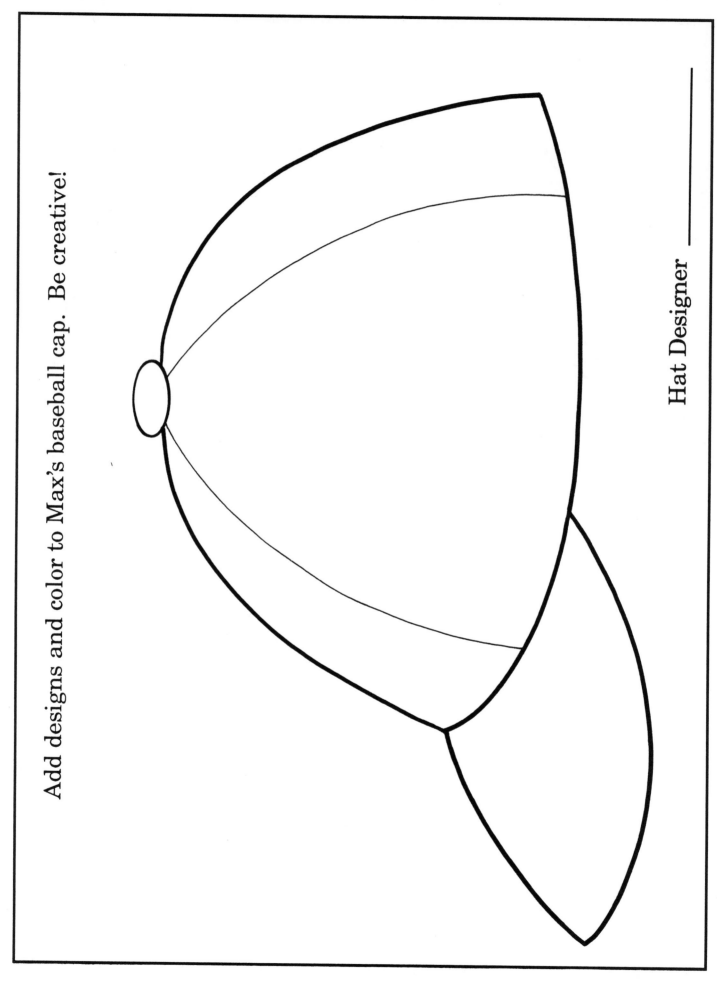

Hat Designer _____

44

GA1427

Name _____

Talent Graph

Reading	Math	Science	Social Studies	Writing	Spelling

Survey people in your school. Ask them to select their greatest talent in school. Record their names in the box in the appropriate column. Color each column to make a bar graph.

Before you begin, predict which column will receive the most responses. _____

Name _____

Exploring the Talent Graph

1. Which column had the most responses?_____
   _____

2. Which column had the least responses?_____
   _____

3. Were there any ties?_____
   _____

4. What conclusions can you make from your graph?____
   _____
   _____
   _____
   _____

5. Was there a difference between boys' and girls' responses? Explain your answer._____
   _____
   _____

6. Something I learned that the graph doesn't show: ___
   _____
   _____
   _____

GA1427

School

HOME-SCHOOL RESEARCH
Talent Train

Home Sweet Home

DIRECTIONS: You are the engineer of a talent train. Discuss your family's talents and record them on the talent ticket below. Using the train shapes, draw a picture of each family member involved in his/her talent. Be sure to label each car. Cut out and assemble into a family talent train.

*This activity could also be completed by students to form a classroom talent train.

Talent Ticket

_____'s talent: _____

_____'s talent: _____

_____'s talent: _____

_____'s talent: _____

_____'s talent: _____

GA1427

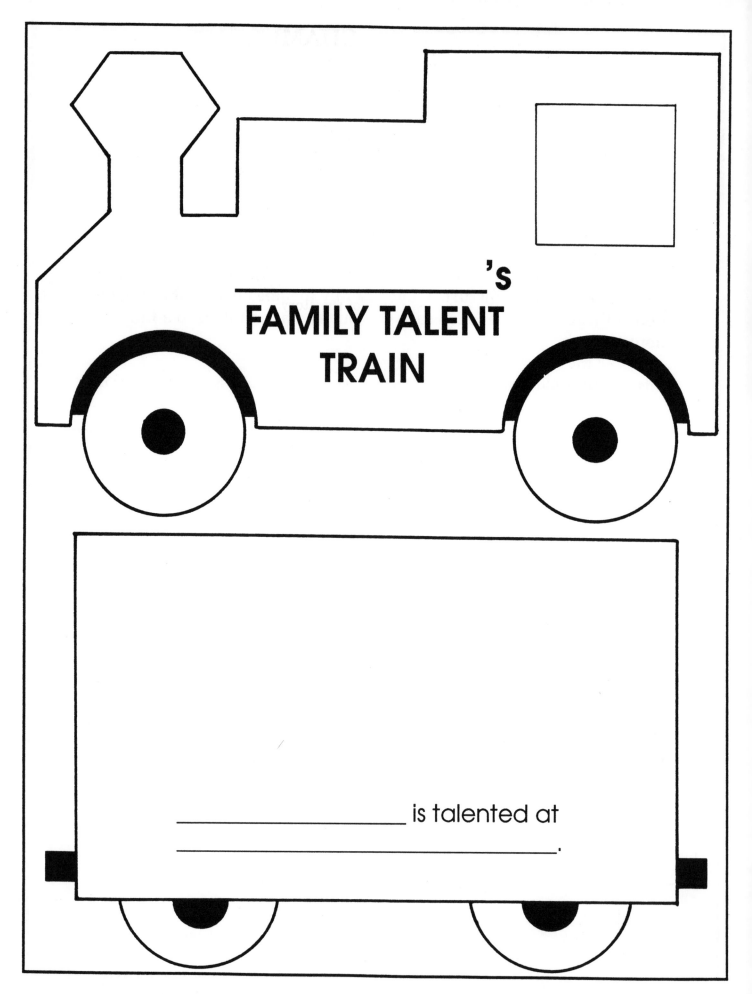

_____'s

FAMILY TALENT TRAIN

_____ is talented at

_____.

48

THE MIXED-UP CHAMELEON

Eric Carle
Harper & Row, NY, 1975

The mixed-up chameleon discovers an important lesson about himself.

BLOOM'S QUESTIONS

KNOWLEDGE
Describe the chameleon at the beginning of the story.

COMPREHENSION
Why did the chameleon want to change?

APPLICATION
If you could have a trait of another person, who and what would it be?

ANALYSIS
How is the mixed-up chameleon like you? How are you the same? How are you different?

*SYNTHESIS
The chameleon is always alone in the story. Create a friend to keep the chameleon company.

EVALUATION
Is the lesson the mixed-up chameleon learned important? Why or why not?

CREATIVE THINKING ACTIVITIES

FLUENCY
List as many physical animal characteristics as you can.

*FLEXIBILITY
Choose one animal characteristic and think of another use for it. Draw your most unusual idea.

ORIGINALITY
Select five or more animal characteristics and create your own one-of-a-kind animal.

ELABORATION
Elaborate on the meaning of the chameleon's comment at the end of the story: "I wish I could be myself."

GA1427

THE MIXED-UP CHAMELEON

50

GA1427

Choose one animal characteristic
and think of another use for it.
Draw your most unusual idea.

Inventor _____

    GA1427

Create a friend to keep the chameleon company. Tell why they are friends and what they like to do together.

Friend _____

52

GA1427

Things-I-Would-Like-to-Change-About-Me Graph

My nose	**My hair**	**My height**	**My weight**	**My eyes**	**Other**

Survey your friends at school. What would they like to change about themselves? Record their names in the box in the appropriate column. Color each column to make a bar graph.

Before you begin, predict which column will receive the most responses. _____

Name _____

Exploring the Things-I-Would-Like-
to-Change-About-Me Graph

1. Which column had the most responses?_____

_____

2. Which column had the least responses?_____

_____

3. Were there any ties?_____

_____

4. What conclusions can you make from your graph?____

_____

_____

_____

_____

5. Why do you think people want to change things
about themselves?_____

_____

_____

_____

6. Create your own graph entitled Things-I-Would-
Like-to-Change-About-the-World Graph. Use the
same format provided.

GA1427

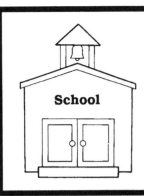

HOME-SCHOOL RESEARCH
Terrific Traits Mobile

Home Sweet Home

School

DIRECTIONS: You are going to create a Terrific Traits Mobile. Interview family members and ask them what traits of yours they would like to have. Then complete four triangles using the shape provided. Be sure to include pictures! Assemble your Terrific Traits triangles as a mobile and display it proudly!

_____'s
Terrific Traits

_____ would like my _____.
(Family Member)   (Terrific Trait)

_____ would like my _____.

_____ would like my _____.

_____ would like my _____.

_____ would like my _____.

_____ would like my _____.

GA1427

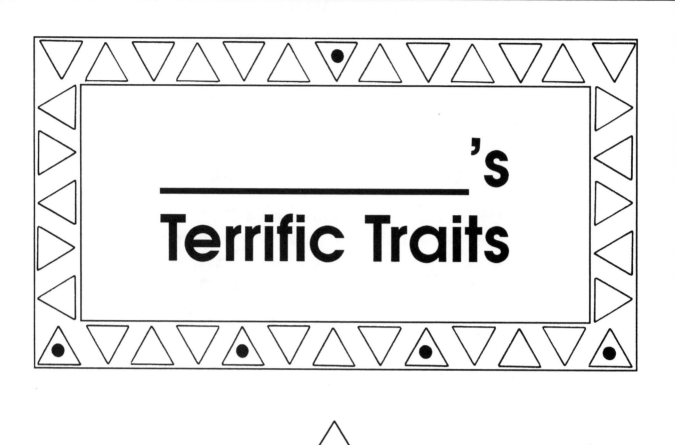

_____'s
Terrific Traits

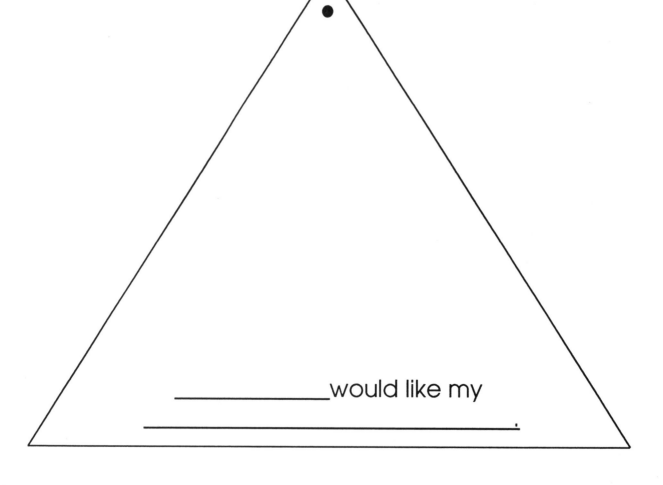

_____ would like my

_____.

56

GA1427

OWLIVER

Robert Kraus
Mulberry Books, NY, 1982

Owliver liked to act all day and all night. His parents thought he was so talented that deciding his career became their goal.

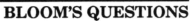

BLOOM'S QUESTIONS

KNOWLEDGE
What is an orphan? Was Owliver an orphan?

COMPREHENSION
Why did Owliver like to act?

APPLICATION
If you were Owliver for the day, what would you act out?

ANALYSIS
How is Owliver's family like your family? How are they alike? How are they different?

*SYNTHESIS
Suppose Owliver had become a doctor. Tell what a typical day would have been like for him.

EVALUATION
Decide whether Owliver's parents were good parents. Why or why not?

CREATIVE THINKING ACTIVITIES

FLUENCY
Brainstorm a long list of careers.

FLEXIBILITY
Divide your career list into the following categories: Indoor Work/Outdoor Work; Work Alone/Work with Others; Careers with Hats/Careers Without Hats.

*ORIGINALITY
Write a letter from Owliver to his parents announcing his decision to become a fire fighter. Be sure to explain Owliver's reasons for choosing this career.

ELABORATION
Elaborate on Owliver's fire fighter's uniform. What else would he need to wear besides a hat?

GA1427

OWLIVER

GA1427

Suppose Owliver had become a doctor.
Tell what a typical day would have been like for him.

Owliver's Schedule

_____
(date)

_____:
(time)

_____:
(time)

_____:
(time)

_____:
(time)

_____:
(time)

_____:
(time)

Doctor _____

Write a letter from Owliver to his parents announcing his decision to become a fire fighter. Be sure to explain Owliver's reasons for choosing this career.

_____
(date)

Dear Mom and Dad,

_____

_____

_____

_____

_____

_____

_____

_____

_____

Your son,
Owliver

GA1427

Name _____

Career Graph

Indoors	**Outdoors**

Work alone	**Work with people**

Survey your friends at school. Ask them about their future careers. Would they like to work indoors or outdoors and with people or alone? Record their names in the box in the appropriate column. Color each column to make a bar graph.

Before you begin, predict which column will receive the most responses. _____

Name _____

Exploring the Career Graph

1. Which column had the most responses?_____

   _____

2. Which column had the least responses?_____

   _____

3. Were there any ties?_____

   _____

4. What conclusions can you make from your graph?_____

   _____

   _____

   _____

   _____

5. Share your future career choice and tell why you
   chose it. _____

   _____

   _____

6. Does your future career choice involve other people?

   _____

   Does your future career choice require you to work
   indoors or outdoors?_____

   _____

GA1427

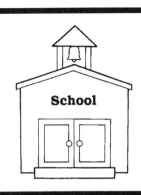

School

HOME-SCHOOL RESEARCH
Color-a-Career

Home Sweet Home

DIRECTIONS: Interview your parents and grandparents. Ask them to share information about three jobs they have held in their lifetime. Also, ask them to tell you about a job of their dreams – one they would like to have. Write your information in the Career Corner below. Next, decide what career best suits *your* talents. Draw a portrait of yourself in the Career Picture Frame.

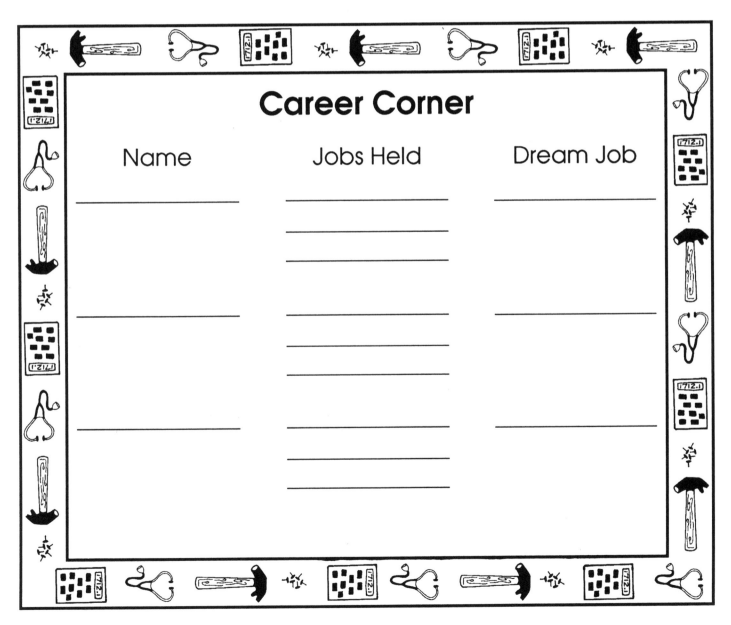

Career Corner

Name	Jobs Held	Dream Job
_____	_____	_____
	_____	
	_____	
_____	_____	_____
	_____	
	_____	
_____	_____	_____
	_____	
	_____	

GA1427

Career Picture Frame

(name)   (career)

64

GA1427

PIGGYBOOK

Anthony Browne
Alfred A. Knopf, NY, 1986

Mrs. Piggot is tired of doing all the household chores for her family. So she disappears and the "men" make an amazing discovery.

BLOOM'S QUESTIONS

KNOWLEDGE
> List three jobs Mrs. Piggot does at her house.

COMPREHENSION
> Why does Mrs. Piggot disappear?

APPLICATION
> Share a time in your life when you were not as helpful as you should have been. Share a time when you felt others were not helpful.

*ANALYSIS
> Compare Mrs. Piggot with your mom. How are they the same? How are they different?

SYNTHESIS
> Predict what would have happened if Mr. Piggot, Patrick, and Simon had not changed when Mrs. Piggot returned.

EVALUATION
> Was it a good idea for Mrs. Piggot to disappear? Why or why not?

CREATIVE THINKING ACTIVITIES

FLUENCY
> Brainstorm a long list of things moms can do.

FLEXIBILITY
> Rank order your five *favorite* things moms do.

*ORIGINALITY
> Mrs. Piggot made a change in her family. Write an announcement for your family bulletin board about a change you would like to make in your family.

ELABORATION
> Through discussion, elaborate on the changes that take place in the Piggot home. Look closely at the illustrations.

GA1427

66

GA1427

Compare Mrs. Piggot with your mom.

Mrs. Piggot	Things in Common	My Mom

Write an announcement for your family bulletin board about a change you would like to make in your family.

Announcer _____

Name _____

Chore Graph

Make bed	**Pick up toys**	**Clear dishes**	**Pick up clothes**	**Brush teeth**	**Other**

Survey people in your school. What chore do they most often remember to complete? Record their names in the box in the appropriate column. Color each column to make a bar graph.

Before you begin, predict which column will receive the most responses. _____

GA1427

Name _____

Exploring the Chore Graph

1. Which column had the most responses? _____
   _____

2. Which column had the least responses? _____
   _____

3. Were there any ties? _____
   _____

4. What conclusions can you make from your graph? _____
   _____
   _____
   _____
   _____

5. Share some of the other chores that appeared in the
   last column. _____
   _____
   _____

6. Bonus Question: What is your favorite chore to do
   at your house? _____
   What is your least favorite chore to do at your
   house? _____

HOME-SCHOOL RESEARCH
Magnificent Mom

Home
Sweet
Home

DIRECTIONS: You are the magnificent son or daughter of a magnificent mom. Brainstorm with your family reasons why your mom is magnificent. Be sure to include your mom in the discussion. Draw or paint a picture of your mom. Then write your five favorite reasons your mom is magnificent from your brainstorming box. Assemble your picture and reasons into a masterpiece that your mom would be proud of. Don't forget to include an appropriate mom border.

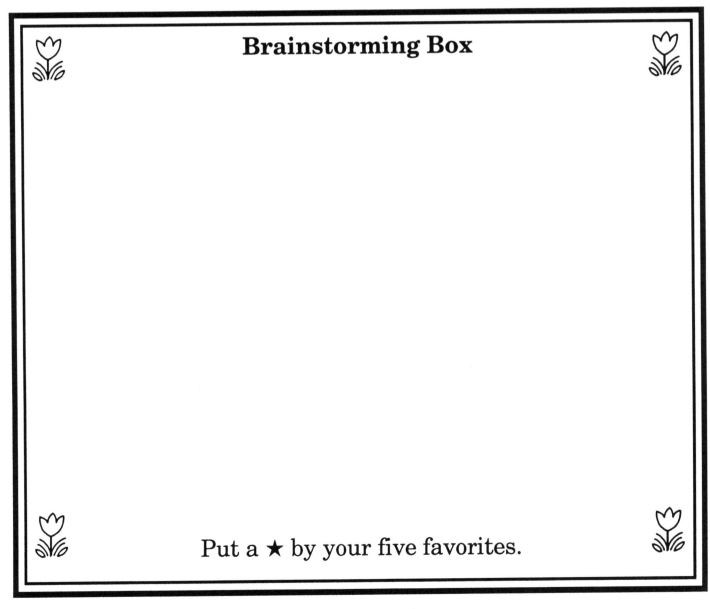

Brainstorming Box

Put a ★ by your five favorites.

GA1427

Magnificent Mom Masterpiece

. . . . Mom Border . . . . .

Mom's
Picture

_____
(Mom's Name)

My mom is magnificent because . . .

1. _____
2. _____
3. _____
4. _____
5. _____

_____
(Your Name)

GA1427

SAY IT!

Charlotte Zolotow
Greenwillow Books, NY, 1980

A mother and daughter share a "magical" autumn day together.

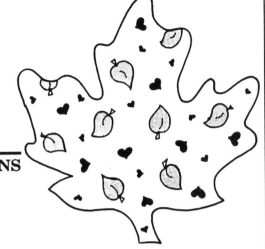

BLOOM'S QUESTIONS

KNOWLEDGE
Describe the setting of the story.

COMPREHENSION
Why did the little girl want to hear her mother say "I love you"?

*APPLICATION
Share a special time you have had with one of your parents.

ANALYSIS
Compare the autumn day in the story with a typical spring day.

*SYNTHESIS
The mother says "I love you" by going for an autumn walk. Draw a picture of a new way to say "I love you."

EVALUATION
Is going on a walk a good way to say "I love you"? Tell why or why not.

CREATIVE THINKING ACTIVITIES

FLUENCY
Brainstorm a long list of autumn words. Use the adjectives in Say It! to get you started.

FLEXIBILITY
Examine your list of autumn words. Decide which words could also describe winter, spring, and/or summer. Place a check next to those words.

ORIGINALITY
Using watercolors, paint your own picture of something you would like to do on a fall day.

ELABORATION
Elaborate on the meaning of the mother's words at the end of the story: "That's what I've been saying all the time."

GA1427

SAY IT!

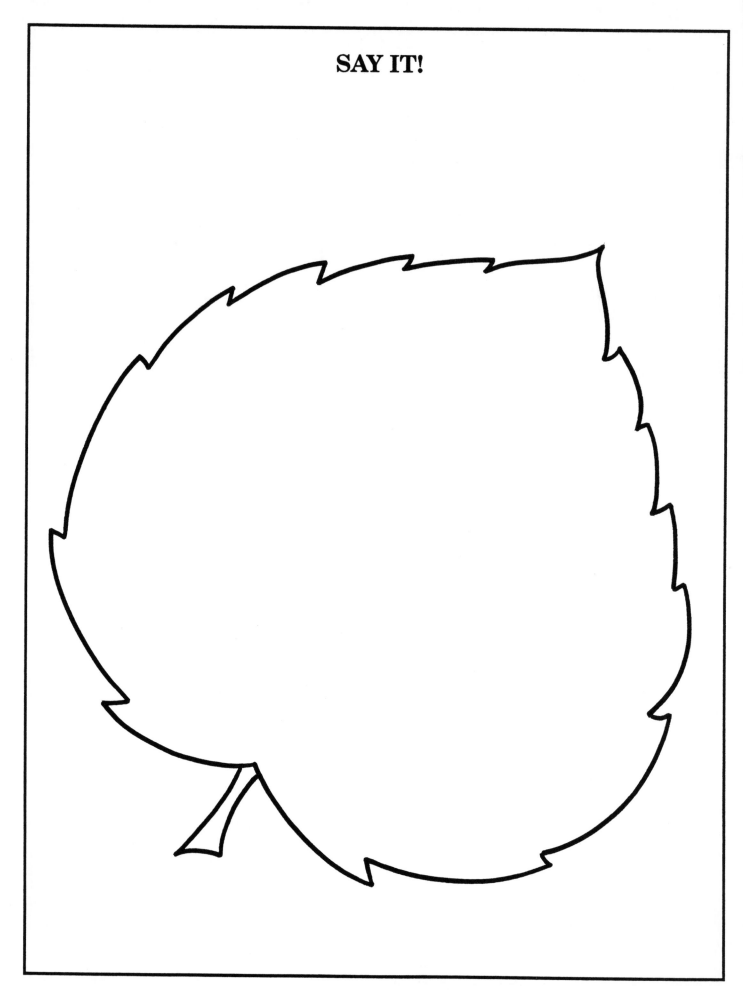

GA1427

SPECIAL TIMES

A special time I had with my _____ was _____
_____ .

We _____

_____

_____

_____

_____

_____

Author _____

GA1427

Draw a picture of a new way to say "I love you."

Loving Person _____

GA1427

Name _____

Ways to Say "I Love You" Graph

Writing a letter	Drawing a picture	Giving a hug	Baking cookies	Doing a chore for someone	Buying a present	Other

Ask people in your school to select a favorite way to say "I love you" from the graph. They must choose only *one* way from the ideas given. Graph the results by writing the name of each person in the boxes. Color each column to make a bar graph.

Before you begin, predict which column will receive the most responses. _____

GA1427

Name _____

Exploring the Ways to Say "I Love You" Graph

1. Which column had the most responses?_____
_____

2. Which column had the least responses?_____
_____

3. Were there any ties?_____
_____

4. What conclusions can you make from your graph?_____
_____
_____
_____

5. Make a list of people and ways you tell them you love them.

People	Ways I Say "I Love You"
Example: <u>Shelby</u>	<u>cuddle and kiss her</u>
_____	_____
_____	_____
_____	_____
_____	_____
_____	_____

GA1427

School

HOME-SCHOOL RESEARCH
Say It! Shout It!

Home Sweet Home

DIRECTIONS: You are going to explore weekend activities with the members of your family. Brainstorm a list of your family's favorite things to do on the weekend. Write your ideas in the box below. Select your favorite activity from the list and draw a picture of it on the "Say It! Shout It!" page.

Weekend Activities

My family's weekend activities are

My favorite weekend activity is

GA1427

Say It! Shout It!

Draw and describe your favorite weekend activity. Make suggestions as to how to make it even better. Assemble your pictures in a class book entitled "Fun Family Weekend Ideas."

My favorite weekend activity is _____
_____ because
_____
_____ .

We could make it even better if _____
_____
_____
_____ .

GA1427

SHY CHARLES

Rosemary Wells
Dial Books, NY, 1988

Charles is very shy and talks to no one. Nothing can get
Charles to open up until an emergency arises.

BLOOM'S QUESTIONS

KNOWLEDGE
  What embarrassed Charles' mother?

COMPREHENSION
  How did Charles save Mrs. Block's life?

APPLICATION
  Charles' father got frustrated with Charles and made him cry. Share a time from
  your own life when you "cried and cried."

ANALYSIS
  Analyze the problems Charles encountered being shy. Discuss the pros and cons.

SYNTHESIS
  Invent a solution to overcome shyness.

EVALUATION
  Was it a good idea for everyone to try to help Charles overcome his shyness? Tell
  why or why not.

CREATIVE THINKING ACTIVITIES

FLUENCY
  Brainstorm situations that make people shy. (Compare your list with those sug-
  gested on the graph.)

FLEXIBILITY
  Everyone focused on Charles' shyness. Look at Charles in another way. List at least
  five other qualities that Charles possesses.

ORIGINALITY
  Make a list of qualities that you possess. Select four qualities that you consider
  strengths. Assemble them into a mobile.

ELABORATION
  Elaborate on what Charles was thinking at the end of the story.

GA1427

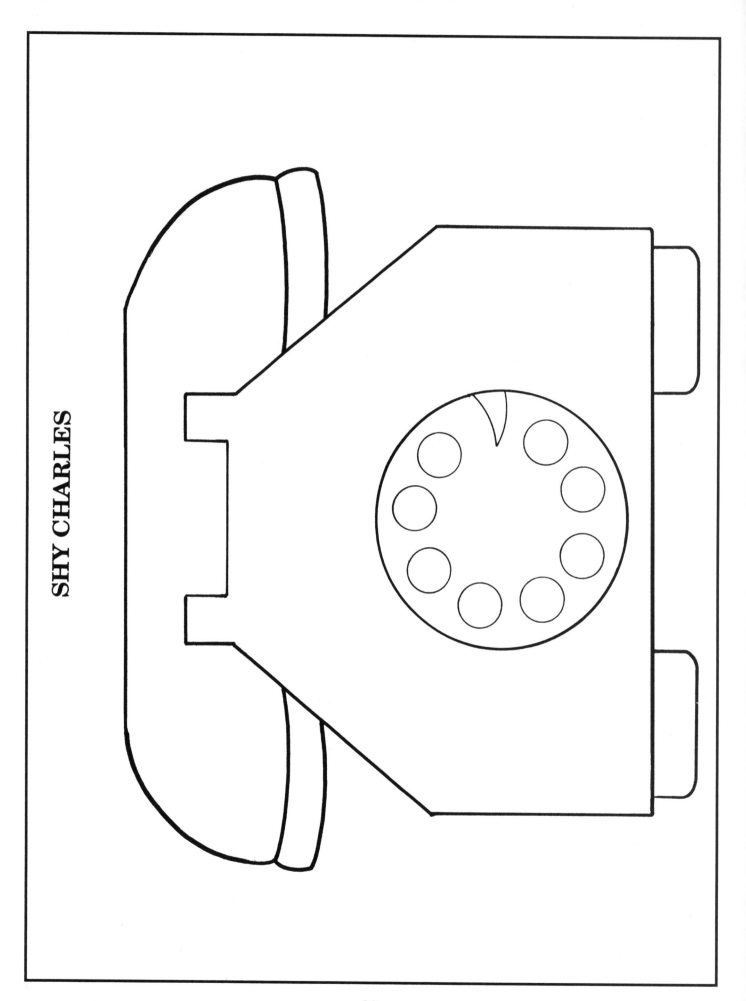

SHY CHARLES

82

GA1427

• BASHFUL • TIMID • SHY • QUIET • BASHFUL • TIMID • SHY • QUIET •

A SHYNESS SOLUTION

My solution for shyness is ______________________________

____

____

____

____

____

____

____

____

____

____

____

____

____

____

____

____

____

____

by ____________________

BASHFUL • TIMID • SHY • QUIET • BASHFUL • TIMID • SHY • QUIET • BASHFUL • TIMID • SHY • QUIET • BASHFUL • TIMID • SHY • QUIET • BASHFUL • TIMID • SHY • QUIET • BASHFUL • TIMID • SHY • QUIET • BASHFUL • TIMID • SHY • QUIET • BASHFUL • TIMID • SHY • QUIET •

MY STRENGTHS MOBILE

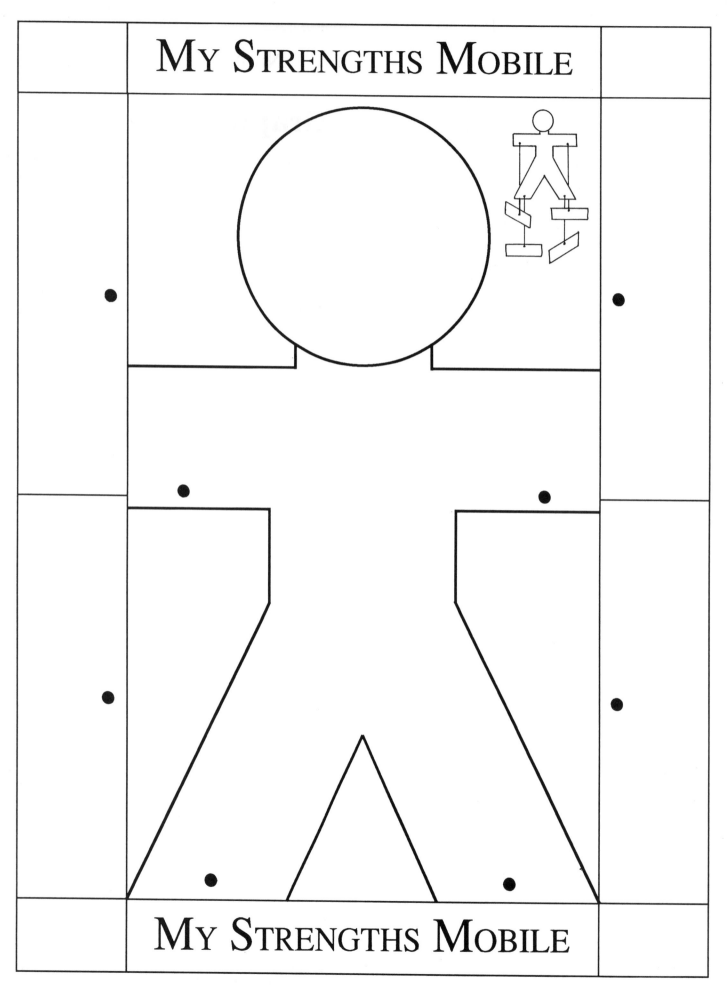

MY STRENGTHS MOBILE

84

GA1427

Name _____

Being-Shy Graph

Meeting new people	Trying a new activity	Speaking in front of a group	Calling on the phone	Going to new places	The first day of school	Other

Survey people in your school. In what situation do they feel most shy? Record their names in the box in the appropriate column. Color each column to make a bar graph.

Before you begin, predict which column will receive the most responses. _____

GA1427

Name _____

Exploring the Being-Shy Graph

1. Which column had the most responses?_____
   _____

2. Which column had the least responses?_____
   _____

3. Were there any ties?_____
   _____

4. What conclusions can you make from your graph?_____
   _____
   _____
   _____
   _____

5. Look at the graph. Which situation makes you feel most shy?_____
   Is there a situation on the graph that doesn't make you feel shy?_____
   Which one?_____

6. Share a time when you felt extremely shy. Describe how it made you feel._____
   _____
   _____

GA1427

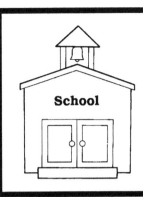

School

HOME-SCHOOL RESEARCH
Home Heroes

Home Sweet Home

DIRECTIONS: You are going to award a blue ribbon to one person in your family. Ask family members to share heroic deeds they have done for the family, such as delivering a forgotten lunch, finding the car keys, helping with homework, etc. Record their responses in the trophy below. Select one deed and award that family member a specially decorated blue ribbon.

GA1427

HEROIC DEED AWARD

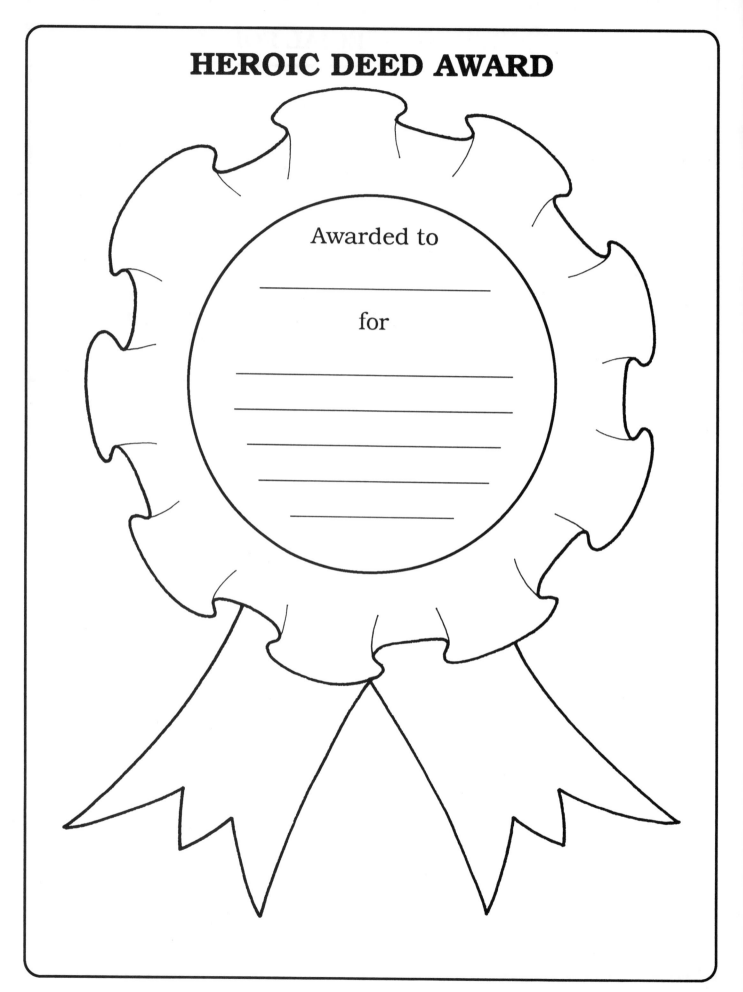

Awarded to

_____

for

_____

_____

_____

_____

_____

SOMETHING SPECIAL FOR ME

Vera B. Williams
Mulberry Books, NY, 1986

Rosa empties the money jar and can buy whatever she wants for her birthday. However, Rosa has difficulty finding just the right present.

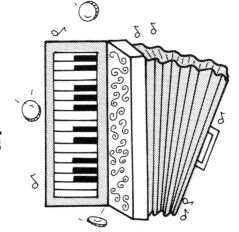

BLOOM'S QUESTIONS

KNOWLEDGE
List three things Rosa thought she wanted to buy.

COMPREHENSION
Why did Rosa finally decide to buy the accordion?

APPLICATION
Share an experience from your life when you had difficulty making a decision.

ANALYSIS
Compare Rosa's birthday experience with one of your birthday experiences. How are they the same? How are they different?

SYNTHESIS
Imagine Rosa had bought one of the first three presents. Write a new ending for the story.

EVALUATION
Was it a good idea for Rosa to have spent all the money at the music store? Why or why not?

CREATIVE THINKING ACTIVITIES

FLUENCY
Make a list of things people save money for.

*FLEXIBILITY
Select one item from your list and write a savings plan for the item.

ORIGINALITY
Rosa used all the money in the money jar for her present. Think of a present for Rosa that would not have cost anything.

*ELABORATION
Elaborate on a birthday hat for Rosa to wear.

GA1427

SOMETHING SPECIAL FOR ME

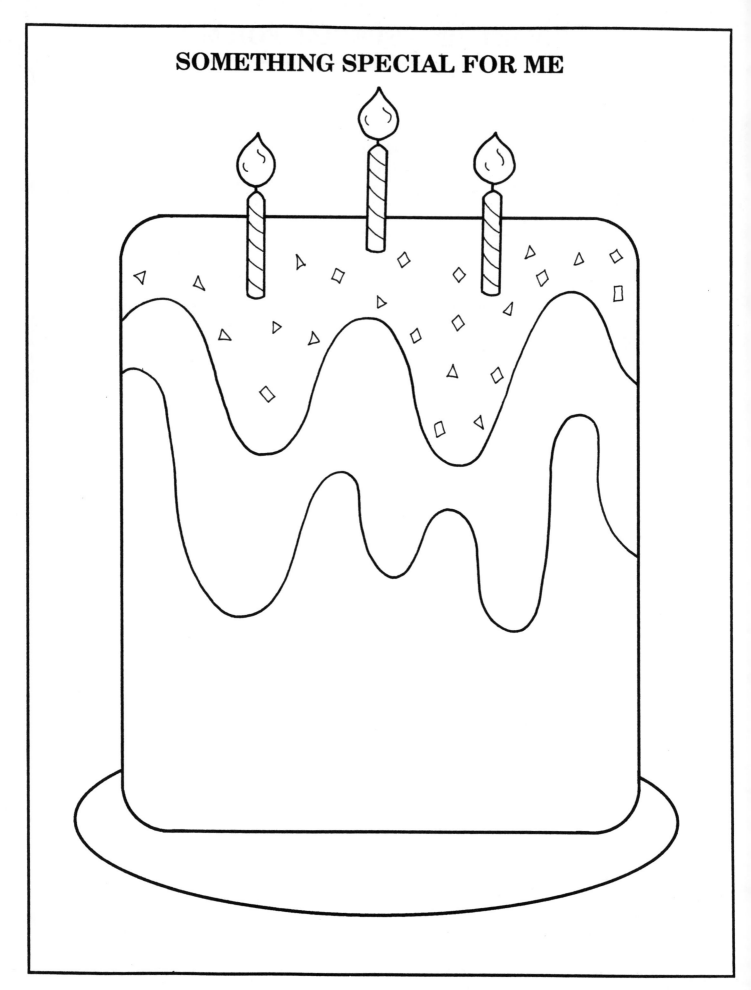

90

GA1427

Something Worth Saving For

I would like to save my money for _____ _____.

I plan to save money by _____, _____, _____, and _____.

(picture of something worth saving for)

Banker _____

GA1427

A Party Hat for Rosa

Create a one-of-a-kind birthday hat for Rosa to wear.

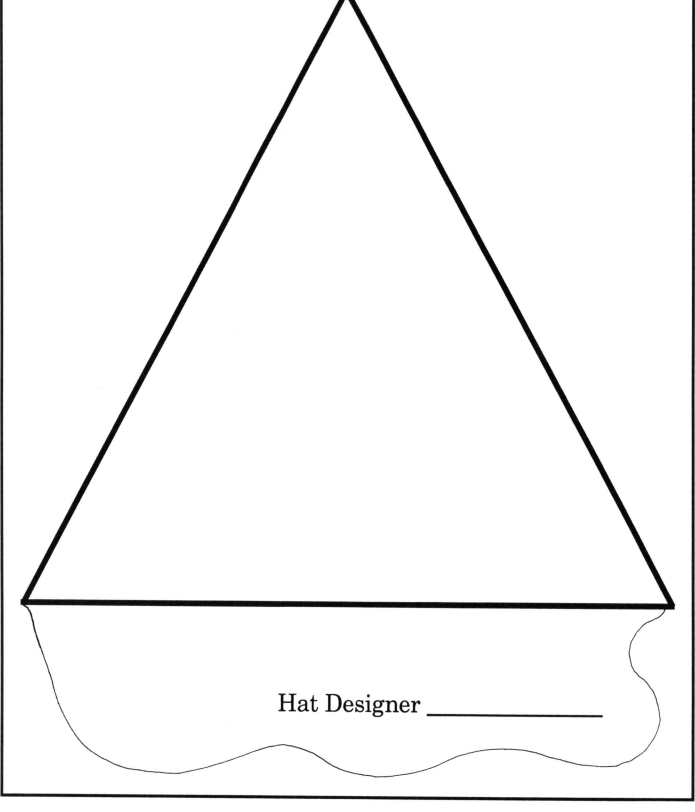

Hat Designer _____

GA1427

Name _____

Ways-to-Earn-Money Graph

Baby-sit	Care for a pet	Rake leaves	Shovel snow	Set table; do the dishes	Household chore	Other

Ask class members to select their favorite ways to earn money from the graph. They must choose only *one* way from the graph. Tally their responses to form a bar graph.

Before you begin, predict which column will receive the most responses. _____

GA1427

Name _____

Exploring the Ways-to-Earn-Money Graph

1. Which column had the most responses?_____
    _____

2. Which column had the least responses?_____
    _____

3. Were there any ties?_____
    _____

4. What conclusions can you make from your graph?____
    _____
    _____
    _____
    _____

5. Did class members share what they were saving
    their money for?_____
    If yes, list their ideas: _____
    _____
    _____
    _____
    _____
    _____

6. What is the largest amount of money you have ever
    saved?_____
    Did you spend this money?_____

GA1427

School

HOME-SCHOOL RESEARCH
A Birthday Postcard

Home
Sweet
Home

DIRECTIONS: Reminisce about a past birthday with a family member. Share the details of your favorite birthday with a grandparent or senior citizen. Tell what you liked about your birthday. Be sure to include details about the cake, presents, decorations, etc. Write a list of things to include on your birthday postcard in the present below. Ask the addressee to respond to your postcard by sharing a favorite birthday of his/her own.

GA1427

My Birthday Postcard

Dear _____

_____

_____

_____

_____

_____

_____

_____

_____

Love, _____

(address)

GA1427

THREE BRAVE WOMEN

C.L.G. Martin
Macmillan Publishing Co., NY, 1991

Caitlin, Mama, and Grammy share a mutual fear of
spiders. Together they conquer their fear and save
Caitlin from embarrassment.

BLOOM'S QUESTIONS

KNOWLEDGE
Tell what Caitlin, Mama and Grammy were each afraid of.

COMPREHENSION
Explain how Caitlin overcame her fear of spiders.

APPLICATION
Share something you are afraid of and how you think you became afraid of it.

ANALYSIS
Compare the three women's reactions to their fears. Which was most embarrassing?
Most dangerous? Most humorous?

SYNTHESIS
If you could have someone looking over your shoulder to protect you when you are
afraid, who or what would it be?

EVALUATION
Is facing your fears a good idea? Why or why not?

CREATIVE THINKING ACTIVITIES

FLUENCY
Brainstorm a list of things people are afraid of.

*FLEXIBILITY
Choose something from your list above and think of five good things about it.

ORIGINALITY
Draw a picture of something that gives you a "giggle fit" to remember.

*ELABORATION
Elaborate on the "I'm Not Afraid Because" poem.

GA1427

THREE BRAVE WOMEN

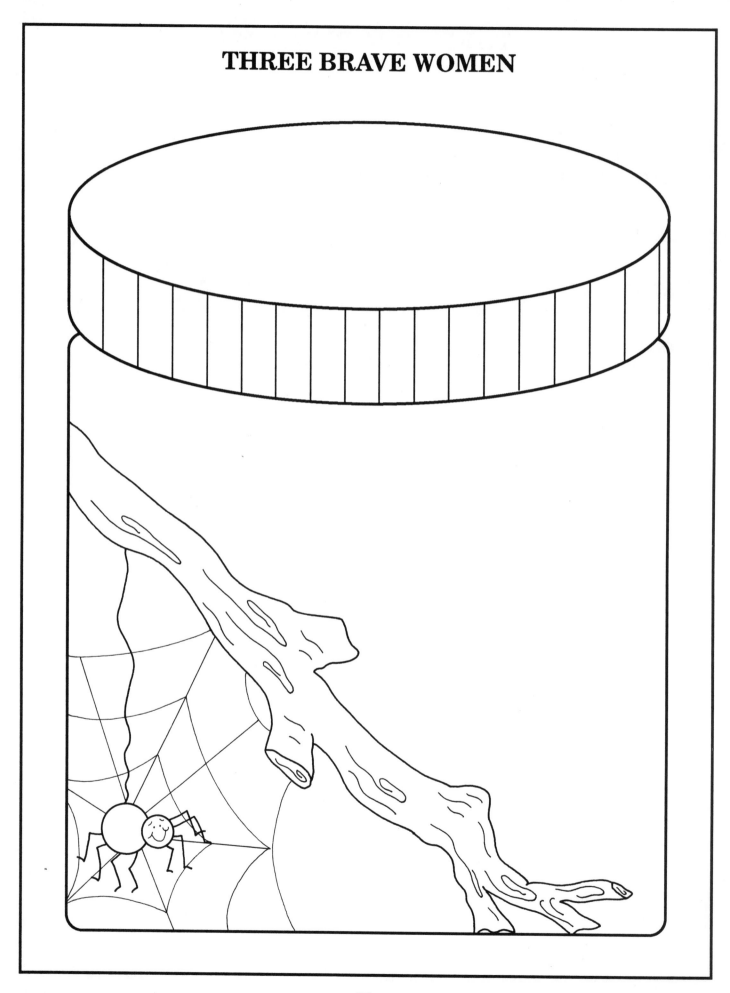

GA1427

On the Bright Side

Something Good About _____

○ 1. _____
   _____

○ 2. _____
   _____

○ 3. _____
   _____

○ 4. _____
   _____

○ 5. _____
   _____

Positive Thinker _____

GA1427

Complete the poem below including three good things about your fear.

I'm Not Afraid Because . . .

Oh, I'm not afraid of _____

No, I'm not afraid of _____

Because _____ are/is

_____

and _____

and _____

Oh, I'm not afraid of _____

No, I'm not afraid of _____

Anymore!

Poet _____

Name _____

Fears Graph

Thunder-storms	**Dark**	**Doctor/ Dentist**	**New situations**	**High places**

Ask people in your school to select their greatest fear from the graph. Record their names in the box in the appropriate column. Color each column to make a bar graph.

Before you begin, predict which column will receive the most responses. _____

GA1427

Name _____

Exploring the Fears Graph

1. Which column had the most responses?_____
   _____

2. Which column had the least responses?_____
   _____

3. Were there any ties?_____
   _____

4. What conclusions can you make from your graph?____
   _____
   _____
   _____
   _____

5. Did someone share a fear other than those listed?____
   What was it?_____
   _____
   _____

6. Did anyone refuse to select a fear from the graph
   stating "I'm not afraid of anything"?_____
   Did you believe them?_____

GA1427

School

HOME-SCHOOL RESEARCH
Family Fears

Home Sweet Home

DIRECTIONS: You are going to investigate and cure your family's fears. Ask each person in your family what he/she is most afraid of. Write the information on the card below. Select one person's fear to record on the "Family Fear Cure" page. Brainstorm solutions to help that person overcome his/her fear.

Family Fear Card

_____ is afraid of _____

_____

_____ is afraid of _____

_____

_____ is afraid of _____

_____

_____ is afraid of _____

_____

_____ is afraid of _____

_____

_____ is afraid of _____

_____

GA1427

FAMILY FEAR CURE

_____'s fear: _____

Possible Solutions:

1. _____
2. _____
3. _____
4. _____
5. _____

Counselor _____

Before

After

Draw a picture of your family member before and after your cure.

GA1427

WE ARE BEST FRIENDS

Aliki
Mulberry Books, NY, 1982

Peter and Robert are best friends. Peter moves away and each boy struggles to adjust to his friend's absence.

BLOOM'S QUESTIONS

KNOWLEDGE
Who moves away in the story?

COMPREHENSION
How does Robert find a new friend?

APPLICATION
Tell about something special you would share with a new friend.

*ANALYSIS
Compare and contrast your interests with one of your classmates.

*SYNTHESIS
Create an original recipe for friendship.

EVALUATION
Are Robert and Peter truly best friends? Tell why or why not.

CREATIVE THINKING ACTIVITIES

FLUENCY
Brainstorm as many ways as you can to make a friend.

FLEXIBILITY
Divide your "Ways to Make a Friend" list into two categories: Ways to Make a Friend Alone and Ways to Make a Friend That Involve Other People.

ORIGINALITY
Design your own stationery and write a letter to a faraway friend. Be sure to tell your friend why you miss him.

ELABORATION
Elaborate on what Robert and Will played at the end of the story.

GA1427

WE ARE BEST FRIENDS

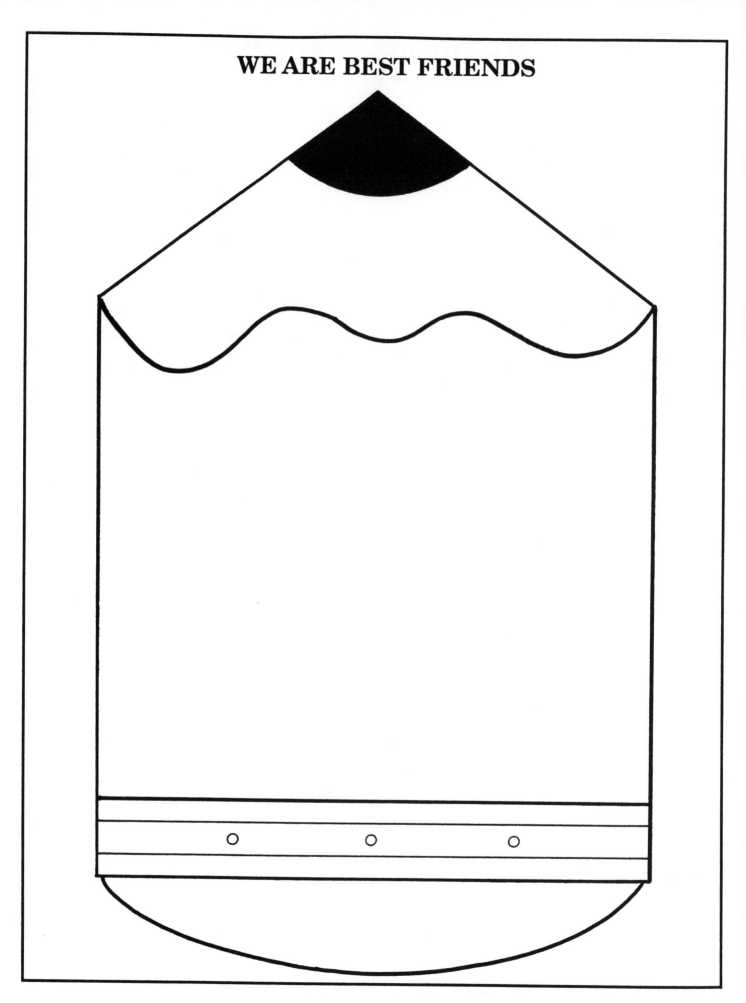

Create an original recipe for friendship.

My Recipe for Friendship

Ingredients _____

_____

_____

_____

Mix _____

_____

_____

_____

Then _____

_____

_____

Bake _____

_____

Chef _____

GA1427

Complete the Interest Venn Diagram listing individual interests of yourself, your classmate, and those you share in common.

Interviewer _____

GA1427

Name _____

Moving Graph

0	**1**	**2**	**3** or more

Survey people in your school. How many good friends have they had move away? Record their names in the box in the appropriate column. Color each column to make a bar graph.

Before you begin, predict which column will receive the most responses. _____

GA1427

Name _____

Exploring the Moving Graph

1. Which column had the most responses?_____

_____

2. Which column had the least responses?_____

_____

3. Were there any ties?_____

_____

4. What conclusions can you make from your graph?_____

_____

_____

_____

_____

5. What was the most difficult part of your data gathering?_____

_____

_____

6. Something I learned that the graph doesn't show:_____

_____

_____

_____

_____

GA1427

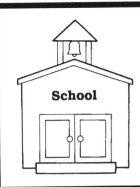

School

HOME-SCHOOL RESEARCH
Neighborhood News

Home
Sweet
Home

DIRECTIONS: You are the star reporter for a neighborhood newspaper. Discuss with your family and/or neighbors newsworthy events that have occurred in your neighborhood recently. These events could include home construction, a celebration, a disaster, etc. Write your ideas in the Reporter's Notebook. Using the newspaper form provided, create a "front page spread."

Reporter's Notebook

Newspaper Names: _____

_____

Neighborhood Headline Events: _____

_____

Picture Possibilities: _____

_____

Editor's Choice: Weather, cartoon, TV listing, horoscope, trivia question, advice column, sports, environmental tip, travel idea, just for fun, movie or book review, health and fitness (This must relate to your neighborhood.)

Circle the choices in each category that you will use on your front page.

GA1427

NEIGHBORHOOD NEWS

_____
name of newspaper

EDITOR-IN-CHIEF: _____

DATE: _____

headline

picture/caption

_____
_____
_____
_____
_____
_____
_____
_____
_____

feature article

editor's choice

GA1427

WILFRID GORDON MCDONALD PARTRIDGE

Mem Fox
Kane/Miller Book Publishers, NY, 1985

Wilfrid befriends Miss Nancy, his neighbor at the old people's home. Together they discover the meaning of a memory.

BLOOM'S QUESTIONS

KNOWLEDGE
Why did Wilfrid like Miss Nancy?

COMPREHENSION
Explain how Wilfrid helped Miss Nancy find her memory.

APPLICATION
Think of one special memory that is as precious as gold to you.

ANALYSIS
How can a memory make you laugh *and* cry?

SYNTHESIS
Think of another way Wilfrid might have helped Miss Nancy find her memory.

EVALUATION
Was Miss Nancy a good friend for Wilfrid? Explain your answer.

CREATIVE THINKING ACTIVITIES

FLUENCY
Brainstorm a list of names in your students' families.

FLEXIBILITY
Play a Jog-Your-Memory game. Someone names an object and others tell what memory it brings back.

*ORIGINALITY
Bring a basket or bag of five of your own memories from home. Complete the tag for the one that is your favorite. Leave this object at school for a classroom Memory Museum.

*ELABORATION
Elaborate on the sentences provided. Then cut and paste them onto pages of a memory book and add illustrations.

GA1427

WILFRID GORDON MCDONALD PARTRIDGE

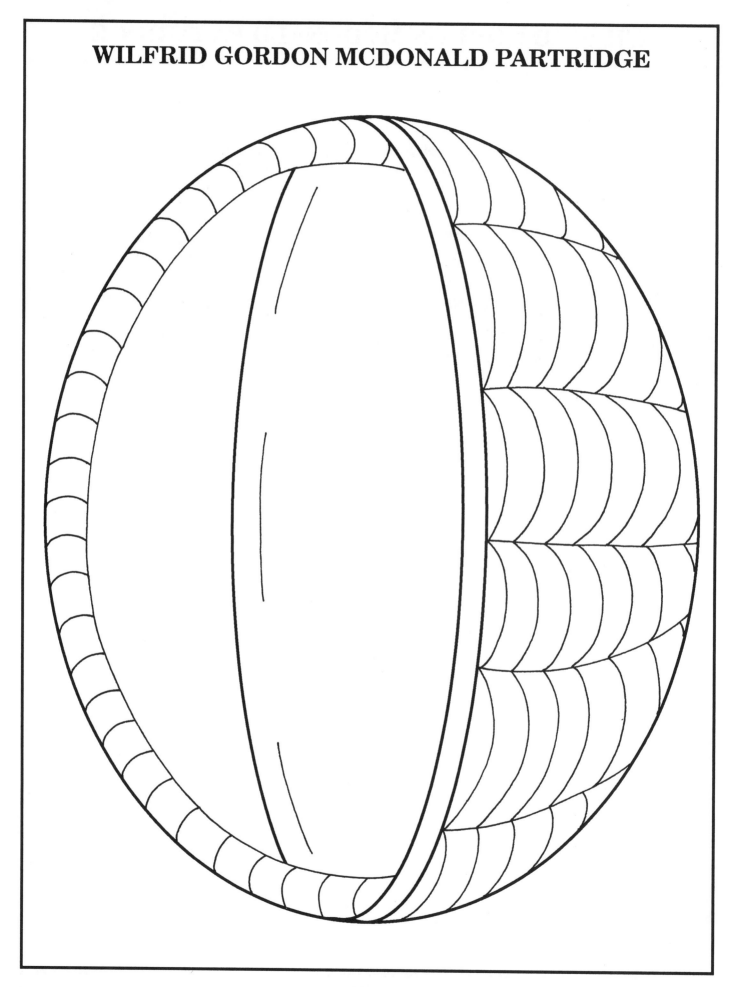

114

GA1427

Complete the Memory Museum tag for your favorite memory object from home.

_____'s Memory

A special memory in my life was _____

_____'s

name

Memory Book

It makes me sad to remember _____
_____
_____ .

It makes me laugh to remember _____
_____
_____ .

It makes me feel warm to remember _____
_____
_____ .

It makes me think of long ago to remember _____
_____
_____ .

Complete the sentences. Cut and paste them onto pages
of a memory book. Add illustrations to each page.

Name _____

Name Graph

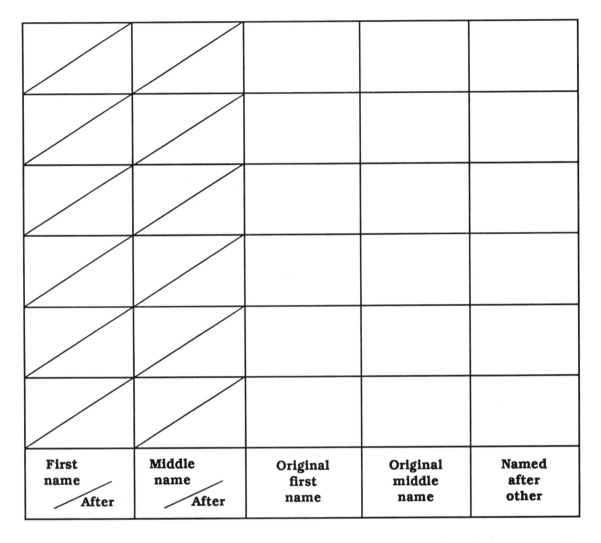

First name / After	Middle name / After	Original first name	Original middle name	Named after other

Survey people in your school. Discover who is named after someone in their family. Record their names in the box in the appropriate column. In the divided boxes, record the name and who they are named after.

Laura / Great-aunt	
First name / After	

Before you begin, predict which column will receive the most responses. _____

GA1427

Exploring the Name Graph

1. Which column had the most responses?_____

   _____

2. Which column had the least responses?_____

   _____

3. Were there any ties?_____

   _____

4. Which name do you think is the most unusual?_____

   _____

   _____

   _____

   _____

5. What was the most interesting story someone
   shared about his/her name?_____

   _____

   _____

6. Did anyone refuse to share his middle name?_____

   _____

   _____

   _____

GA1427

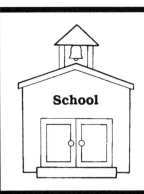

HOME-SCHOOL RESEARCH
Family Names

Home Sweet Home

DIRECTIONS: You are going to research the meanings of your family members' names. Ask your parents to help you complete the name chart below. Try to fill in as many blanks as you can. Now choose at least four people to include in your Family Name Dictionary.

Name Chart

Wanda
Alvin   Dick
Rebecca   Lula May
Harry

Grace
Leah   Edward
Fred   Eleanor
James

My Name _____ _____ _____

Father _____ _____ _____

Mother _____ _____ _____

Sibling _____ _____ _____

Sibling _____ _____ _____

Grandmother _____ _____ _____

Grandfather _____ _____ _____

Grandmother _____ _____ _____

Grandfather _____ _____ _____

GA1427

My Family Name Dictionary

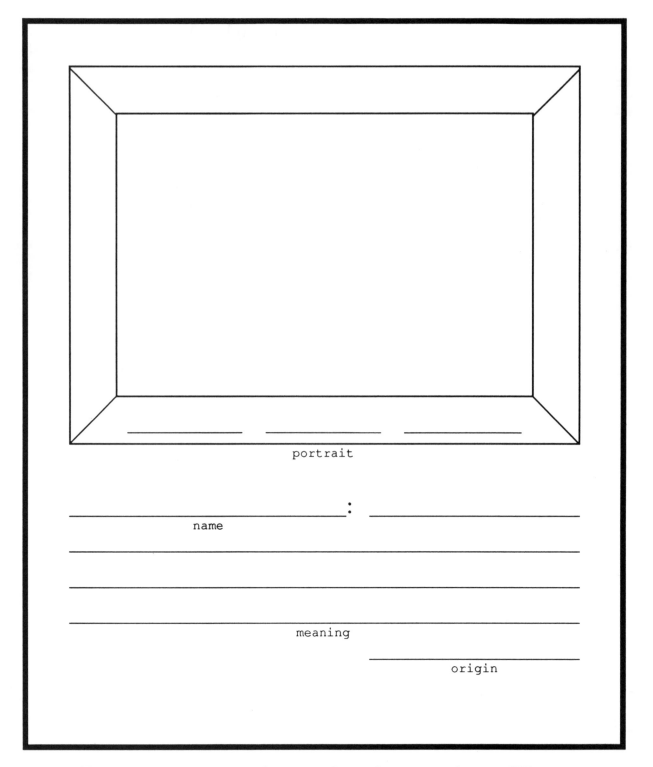

portrait

_____ : _____

name

_____

_____

_____

meaning

                                    _____

                                    origin

Draw a picture of your family member. Write
the whole name in the frame. Select one of the
names and write its meaning.

GA1427

Bibliography

Aliki. *We Are Best Friends*. New York: Mulberry Books, 1982.

Browne, Anthony. *Piggybook*. New York: Alfred A. Knopf, 1986.

Carle, Eric. *The Mixed-Up Chameleon*. New York: Harper & Row, 1975.

Fox, Mem. *Wilfrid Gordon McDonald Partridge*. New York: Kane/Miller Book Publishers, 1985.

Gauch, Patricia Lee. *Christina Katerina and the Time She Quit the Family*. New York: G.P. Putnam's Sons, 1987.

Henkes, Kevin. *Julius • The Baby of the World*. New York: Greenwillow Books, 1990.

Isadora, Rachel. *Max*. New York: Collier Books, 1976.

Kraus, Robert. *Leo the Late Bloomer*. New York: Windmill Books, 1971.

Kraus, Robert. *Owliver*. New York: Mulberry Books, 1982.

Martin, C.L.G. *Three Brave Women*. New York: Macmillan Publishing Co., 1991.

GA1427

Otey, Mimi. *Daddy Has a Pair of Striped Shorts*. New York: Farrar, Straus and Giroux, 1990.

Wells, Rosemary. *Shy Charles*. New York: Dial Books, 1988.

Williams, Vera B. *Something Special for Me*. New York: Mulberry Books, 1986.

Zolotow, Charlotte. *The Hating Book*. New York: Harper & Row, 1969.

Zolotow, Charlotte. *Say It!* New York: Greenwillow Books, 1980.

GA1427